Dennis Marc Busch

Dynamic Content and Format

GRIN Publishing

Bibliographic information published by the German National Library:

The German National Library lists this publication in the National Bibliography; detailed bibliographic data are available on the Internet at http://dnb.dnb.de .

Imprint:

Copyright © 2004 GRIN Verlag GmbH
Print and binding: Books on Demand GmbH, Norderstedt Germany
ISBN: 978-3-638-89637-5

This book at GRIN:

http://www.grin.com/en/e-book/44365/dynamic-content-and-format

GRIN - Your knowledge has value

Since its foundation in 1998, GRIN has specialized in publishing academic texts by students, college teachers and other academics as e-book and printed book. The website www.grin.com is an ideal platform for presenting term papers, final papers, scientific essays, dissertations and specialist books.

Seminar
Document Engineering
Dynamic Content and Format

06.12.2004

Institut für Softwaretechnologie
Fakultät für Informatik
Universität der Bundeswehr München

Contents

1 "XML is text, but isn't meant to be read"

Number three in World Wide Web Consortium's (W3C) "XML in 10 points"
[W3C, 2001] pinpoints one main feature and problem of XML languages.
They only describe the contained information based on structural aspects,
and separate it from the design. In order to present this information, for
example as a web page or in print, they have to be transformed into an
appropriate form.

XSL is an concept for expressing stylesheets that can transform XML
documents. This term paper provides an overview over the main concepts
of transforming XML with XSL, describes another representative of generic
markup, LaTeX and shows, how these concepts can be brought together into
practice.

2 XSL

The Extensible Stylesheet Language (XSL) is a family of languages for defining XML document transformations specified by W3C. It consists of three
parts:

- XSL Transformations (XSLT): a language for transforming XML documents

- XML Path Language (XPath): an expression language used to access
  or refer nodes of XML documents

- XSL Formatting Objects (XSL-FO): a language for defining formatting
  semantics

2.1 XSLT

The Extensible Stylesheet Language Transformations (XSLT) is a language
for transforming XML documents into another form like HTML, plain text,
LaTeX or a different XML language. Every transformation process includes
three documents:

- the source document, which has to be an XML document and contains
  the information

- the stylesheet, containing the instructions, describing how the source
  document has to be transformed, and

- the resulting document, that is generated in the transformation process.

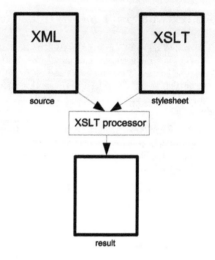

Figure 1: Interrelation in XSLT process

The interrelation between these three documents is shown in figure 1. An XSLT processor uses the rules of the stylesheet to transform the source document into the resulting document.

Stylesheets contain various commands sorted in three groups according to the stylesheet-hierarchie(cp. [Bongers, 2004] p. 32):

- *Root elements* act as the root of the stylesheet. There are only two possibilities for root elements: `xsl:stylesheet` and `xsl:transform` which are used synonymical, and there is only one of them per stylesheet.

- *Top-level elements* are directly subordinated to the root element. XSLT 2.0 contains 16 top-level elements like templates, declaration of functions, parameters, and formatting rules.

- *Instructions* are inferior non-global commands like template calls, constraints, loops, etc. XSLT 2.0 knows about 31 elements of this group.

The following example is to illustrate this approach.

Firstly we assume a very simple source document (see figure 2). As one can see, it's adequate that the source is well-formed, it does not have to follow a specific DTD or XML scheme.

```
<?xml version="1.0"?>
<shout>XSL is great!</shout>
```

Figure 2: example.xml

```
<?xml version="1.0"?>
<xsl:stylesheet version="2.0" xmlns:xsl="http://www.w3c.org/1999/XSL/Transform">
<xsl:template match="/">
  <html>
  <body>
    <h1>Let's shout:</h1>
    <p><xsl:value-of select="shout"/></p>
  </body>
  </html>
</xsl:template>
</xsl:stylesheet>
```

Figure 3: example.xsl

The second needed document is the stylesheet (see figure 3).

It consists of two main tags: XSL commands, marked by the XML namespace pattern xsl:, and literal result elements, the tags not containing xsl: in the example. While XSL commands define actions to be executed by the processor the literal result elements will be passed on unchanged in the result document. The following passage is to give the reader a closer look at the important parts of the example.

<xsl:stylesheet (...)> represents the root element of the stylesheet. Enclosed attributes are the XSLT version (here: 2.0) and the XML namespace declaration for XSL.

<xsl:template match="/"> is the most important top-level element. Normally there is more than one template per stylesheet, but it isn't nessecary in this case. The attribute match="/" is an XPath pattern, that declares when it should be applied (see section 2.2). Here it matches "/", the document root of the source (which is the top level in every XML document and encloses the whole document). So the processor got its starting point. It instantiates the template in the result document and writes the literal result elements like <html> without changes.

When it reaches the instruction <xsl:value-of select="shout"/>, the processor executes it at exactly this point. xsl:value-of generates text being taken from the source. This text concludes from the interpreted XPath expression of the select attribute. It tells the processor to take the value of the element called `<shout>` and to put it into the result. Then it writes out the other literal result elements and finishes the transforming process. You can see the result in figure 4.

```
<html>
<body>
  <h1>Let's shout:</h1>
  <p>XSL is great!</p>
</body>
</html>
```

Figure 4: example.html

As one can see, the example above contains a representative of each of the XSLT command groups; the root element `xsl:stylesheet`, the top-level element `xsl:template`, and the instruction `xsl:value-of`.

Though this is a very simple example the reader should not underestimate the mightiness of XSLT. It is very powerful and provides the possibility for example to generate whole tables of contents, SVG graphics or even LATEX files.

2.2 XPath

XPath is a subset of the XML Query Language (XQuery) and provides the vocabulary for addressing parts of a XML document. XPath uses a tree based, UNIX filesystem-like view on the document. It assumes a syntax similar to URIs where elements or attribute qualifiers are separated by slashes (/). So-called XPath location steps consist of two components, *axis specifier* and *node test*: `axisspecifier::nodetest()`.

The *Axis Specifier* indicates the direction and range of moves in the document tree which are called *axes*. XPath knows 13 axes with various directions and ranges, for example `child::`, which is the specifier for children of an element, or `descendant::`, which selects all successors of an element up to the leafs. More axis specifiers are shown in table 1 in appendix A.

The *node test* selects a subset of nodes defined by the axis specifier, filtering nodes that satisfy the criterias of the node test. Node tests can be for example `text()`, that selects text nodes, `comment()`, that selects comment nodes, or explicit named nodes like `nodename`, which selects every node in the axis.

The following location step is employed to make the reader understand this: `/descen-dant::p`. We apply it to the example HTML document in figure 4 (that is possible, because the documents also fulfils the XHTML standard - so it is an XML document). The following results: the parser begins at the document root (/); the declared axis is `descendant::` so all nodes inferior to the root are selected (that means `html`, `body`, `h1`, and `p`). The node test is `p`, that means only nodes named "p" pass the rule. So the result of this step is the node `<p>XSL is great!</p>`.

XPath provides a possibility to shorten expressions. This was already shown in figure 3. The instruction `<xsl:value-of select="shout"/>` contains the XPath pattern `shout`. The `child::` axis is the default, because it is the most used. So in long form the pattern means `child::shout`. It matches the `shout` node, because the template was applied to document root by its argument `match="/"`. Some other common shortcuts are listed in table 2 in appendix A.

Location Steps can be extended by constraints. Constraint expressions follow a node test and are typed within [ ] braces. Constraints select nodes for which the test expression gives true. They may contain arithmetic (`+ - * div mod`), boolean operators (`or` and `!` `<` `>` `<=` `>=` `=` `!=`) and/or various functions. For example, the (shortened) XPath expression `/p[string ="XSL is poor!"]` applied again to the HTML example in figure 4 would not result in the `p` node, because the the test concerning the string value of the node gives false.

2.3 XSL-FO

XSL Formatting Objects (XSL-FO) is a XML language for generating layouts out of XML documents. The target of the layout is a presentation on paper or monitor. It extends the XSL process. The process again starts with a source XML document. Then an XSLT transformation is applied (using a stylesheet) to select parts or the whole document content and to create an output XML document using the XSL-FO vocabulary. This XSL-FO stylesheet describes how the content of the document should be laid out for presentation (cp. [Pawson, 2002] p. 9). Finally a formatter interprets the XSL-FO stylesheet to produce formatted output, today most commonly Adobe's Portable Document Format (PDF).

Base of every XSL-FO document is `<fo:root>`. Child elements are one `<fo:layout-master-set>`, a optional `<fo:declarations>` and at least one `<fo:page-sequence>` element. In the `<fo:layout-master-set>` the page layout is declared, like page size, headers, margins etc.`<fo:declarations>` elements allow to lay out colour profiles, but they are rarely used because hardly any formatter supports them yet. The `<fo:page-sequence>` elements map out the order of appearance of the pages defined in `<fo:layout-master-set>` (cp. [Pineda and Krüger, 2004] p. 65).

Figure 5 shows a brief sample of a XSL-FO document. `<fo:layout-mas-ter-set>` here contains `<fo:simple-page-master>` with the name only. Because no values for sizes etc. are given, default values are assumed. `<fo:region-body/>` sets up the page body appearance, only with defaults as well. `<fo:page-sequence>` references to the `<fo:simple-page-master>` template. `<fo:flow>` contains the actual content of the document. A `<fo:block>` is the basic element of the content, for example a paragraph. Given to a formatter the output document would simply contain the text "XSL-FO is great!" formatted with the formatter's defaults (cp. [Pineda and Krüger, 2004] p. 65f.).

```
<?xml version="1.0">
<fo:root xmlns:fo="http://www.w3c.org/1999/XSL/Format">
  <fo:layout-master-set>
    <fo:simple-page-master master-name="only">
      <fo:region-body/>
    </fo:simple-page-master>
  </fo:layout-master-set>
  <fo:page-sequence master-reference="only">
    <fo:flow flow-name="xsl-region-body">
      <fo:block>XSL-FO is great!</block>
    </fo:flow>
  </fo:page-sequence>
</fo:root>
```

Figure 5: Simple XSL-FO example

2.4 CSS - An Alternative To XSL?

Cascading Stylesheets (CSS) are like XSL a specification of the W3C. Both can help solving the presentation problem of XML documents but use different approaches. While XSL transforms documents into others (e.g. XML → HTML), that contain the information, how to present it, CSS is used together with a document and defines, how XML elements should be formatted without changing the source.

> XSL uses a XML notation, CSS uses its own. In CSS, the formatting object tree is almost the same as the source tree, and inheritance of formatting properties is on the source tree. In XSL, the formatting object tree can be radically different from the source tree, and inheritance of formatting properties is on the formatting object tree. [Kreulich, 2003]

Syntax is based on single rules that consist of a selector and and one or more declarations. Selectors choose elements (e.g. HTML tags); declarations assign properties and values to these elements. Cascading Stylesheets can inherit rules from each other or other sources.

```
shout {
    font-style: bold;
    color: red;
    background-color: white;
}
```

Figure 6: example.css

In figure 6 a very simple CSS is shown. It contains only one rule: to all elements named `shout` the declarations in { } are assigned, where properties and values are separated by ":" while declarations themselves are separated by ";". To apply this CSS to our first example XML document (figure 2) a xml-stylesheet processing instruction has to be added to the XML file: `<?xml-stylesheet href="example.css" type="text/css"?>`.[1] When the document is viewed in a web browser, it shows the content of the element `shout` bold, in red colour, and on a white background. One can see, unlike an XSL transformation, the source documents leaves untouched (apart from the processing instruction).

So let us give an answer to the question wether CSS is an alternative to XSL. Is is not. It is a complement. Although you can assign simple designs to XML documents, CSS is not able to fit the structure of an XML document to publishing standards; it lacks of possibilities to rearrange or transform elements. But CSS offers a way to make the design of web sites easyer by splitting design from design templates and centralise these. That enables quick and easy changes of the design without changing for example XSL stylesheets.

3 LaTeX

LaTeX is a set of macros for the TeX typesetting system.

It offers programmable desktop publishing features and extensive facilities for automating most aspects of typesetting and desktop publishing, including numbering and cross-referencing, tables and figures, page layout, bibliographies, and much more.

---

[1] To apply a CSS to a HTML 4.0 (not XHTML) document you must use `<LINK href="example.css" rel="stylesheet" type="text/css">`.

LaTeX was originally written in 1984 by Leslie Lamport and has become the dominant method for using TeX; few people write in plain TeX any more. (from Wikipedia, the free encyclopedia)

```
\section{XSL}
The Extensible Stylesheet Language (...) consists of three parts:
\begin{itemize}
    \item XSL Transformations (XSLT)
    \item XML Path Language (XPath)
    \item XSL Formatting Objects (XSL-FO)
\end{itemize}
```

Figure 7: example.tex

Figure 7 shows a part of the beginning of this term paper in its LaTeX source. `\section{XSL}` starts a new section with the parameter (later caption) "XSL". Then follows normal text. `\begin{itemize}` and `\end{itemize}` form a so-called environment that generates a list in which the `\item` command starts a list item. All settings that effect the whole document are declared in the document header which at least has to contain the `\documentclass` command that assigns the document to a document class with its particular defaults. In this paper it is `\documentclass[11pt,a4paper,twoside]{article}` which semantic should be obvious.

Like XML, LaTeX uses a generic markup syntax to tag structural information in documents. But unlike XML LaTeX was conceived especially to mark up the structure of text documents for printing requirements and is not applicable to model any other kind of information. LaTeX documents are always transformed into printable formats like Postscript (PS) or PDF.

Although it is very popular among, and most commonly used by mathematicans and scientists, LaTeX is not perfect for manual use; creatng complex layouts is difficult and not very efficient compared to visual desktop publishing tools. [2] Its full power can be used in automatic document generation (see next section).

Compared to XSL-FO LaTeX can be an alternative - in this case the XML documents are transformed into LaTeX documents and from there to PS or PDF. Or it can be a complement when an XSL-FO formatter is used to build LaTeX code. Which of these options makes sense depends on the considered aim of the process.

---

[2]like Adobe's PageMaker or Microsoft's Publisher

4 Joining All Together

All of the shown concepts have their specific field of application. Brought together, synergic effects turn them into a very efficient system for creating, using and archiving documents. To illustrate this thread imagine you have got to implement a web portal. A few years ago the classical approach was to code the pages of the site in static HTML. That brings a lot of problems - changing the design of the site forces you to change every single HTML page. The solution here is the use of CSS. All of your HTML pages can reference one single CSS. If you sell the portal to another company you just have to change this file to overtake the corporate identity.

The new company wants to provide the contents for customers in PDF format so that they can easily save and print the documents.[3] Without XSL it would have to convert every document to PDF - and again on every change of the document. Informations would have to be stored redundantly. Introducing a XSL infrastructure allows you to save documents in XML format. If a customer requests a web page, a XSLT processor creates HTML code that again can refer to a CSS and include its benefits. If now the customer wants to print the page you can let the XSLT processor apply another XSL stylesheet to create a XSL-FO document, which is transformed into PDF by a XSL-FO formatter. If you want to use LaTeX because of its surpassing capabilities in typesetting mathematical formulas you can just change the XSLT stylesheet again and let the XSLT processor produce LaTeX code that can be transformed into PS or PDF.

5 Conclusion

Using dynamic document generation includes strict seperation of content and design. So changes in design or content normally only effect one single document. This makes this appraoch more efficient the more documents are in use.

Of course, the possible applications cover much more than web portals; every process creating, using, storing and changing documents can take advantage of migration to XML/XSL.

Although attention should hereby be paid to the higher implementation costs, companies dealing with big amounts of documents here gain high savings potential when using dynamic document generation with XSL, CSS and (optional) LaTeX.

---

[3]Results of printing web pages are nearly unpredictable in the light of countless possibilities for combinations of monitor resolutions, printers, browsers, etc.

A   Appendix

Table 1: Example XPath Axis Specifiers

specifier	selected nodes
self	the current node
child	children of the current node
descendant	all descendants of the current node
parent	parents of the current node
anchestor	all ancestors of the current node
attribute	attribute nodes

Table 2: Common XPath Shortcuts

expression	shortcut
child::test	test
self::node()	.
parent::node()	..
descendant-or-self::node()	//
attribute::	@

References

Frank Bongers. *XSLT 2.0 - Das umfassende Handbuch*. Galileo Computing, Bonn, 1. edition, 2004.

Klaus Kreulich. Xml formatting objects - medienunabhängige dokumentaufbereitung, Jan 2003. URL http://makeashorterlink.com/?U6D32310A. Fetched Dec 5th 2004.

Dave Pawson. *XSL-FO - Making XML Look Good in Print*. O'Reilly, Sebastopol, CA (USA), 1. edition, 2002.

Manuel Montero Pineda and Manfred Krüger. *XSL-FO in der Praxis - XML-Verarbeitung für PDF und Druck*. dpunkt.verlag, Heidelberg, 1. edition, 2004.

W3C. Xml in 10 points, Nov 2001. URL http://www.w3.org/XML/1999/XML-in-10-points. Fetched Dec 5th 2004.